Instant EdgeSight for XenApp

Effective, practical instructions to monitor your
Citrix XenApp servers using EdgeSight 5.4

Vaqar Hasan

PUBLISHING

BIRMINGHAM - MUMBAI

Instant EdgeSight for XenApp

First published: August 2013

Production Reference: 1230814

Published by Packt Publishing Ltd.
Livery Place
35 Livery Street
Birmingham B3 2PB, UK.

ISBN 978-1-84968-958-8

www.packtpub.com

Credits

Author
Vaqar Hasan

Reviewers
Ferdinand Feenstra
Kevin Howell

Acquisition Editors
Usha Iyer
Julian Ursell

Commissioning Editor
Neha Nagwekar

Technical Editors
Hardik B. Soni
Veena Pagare

Project Coordinator
Joel Goveya

Proofreader
Stephen Copestake

Production Coordinator
Prachali Bhiwandar

Cover Work
Prachali Bhiwandar

Cover Image
Valentina Dsilva

About the Author

Vaqar Hasan is an IT Consultant living in Toronto, Canada. He holds a Bachelor's degree in Computer Science. He also holds a degree in Commerce and has many certifications from vendors such as Citrix, Microsoft, VMware, CompTIA, Exin, and Apple. He is a Citrix Certified Enterprise Engineer and an Administrator (CCEE and CCEA). His main focus of interest has been Citrix and the VMware technologies.

Vaqar loves to do consulting and has been engaged with companies having one of the largest IT infrastructures in Canada, such as Bell, Service Alberta, and Bank of Nova Scotia.

I would like to dedicate this book to my late parents, Irshad Hasan and Saleha Khatoon.

I would also like to dedicate this book to my wife, Mahira, for helping me spare enough time at home to complete this book.

I wish to thank the reviewers and the team at Packt Publishing, especially Joel and Neha, for their support and belief in me.

About the Reviewers

Ferdinand Feenstra is a Citrix Certified Architect and a senior specialist for Microsoft environments, based in The Netherlands. He has been working in IT since 1998 and is experienced in many complex environments with different customers in various functions.

His experience can be categorized under building and designing Citrix environments, implementing and migrating projects, and consultancy projects. Ever since he discovered working with Citrix in 2004, a new world of solutions—working on any device combined with great user experience—has opened up to him. Citrix makes IT more dynamic and easier to adopt for users. You can find his blog at www.CitrixGuru.net or check his tweets on Twitter at @f_feenstra.

This is the fourth book that he has reviewed. He has already reviewed *XenServer 6.0 Administration Essential Guide, Daniele Tosatto, Packt Publishing*; *XenDesktop 5.6 Cookbook, Gaspare A. Silvestri, Packt Publishing*; and *Implementing Citrix XenServer Quickstarter, Gohar Ahmed, Packt Publishing*.

Ferdinand works for Icento. Icento is a Citrix Partner Solution Advisor with the Silver status. Icento is also a member of V-Alliance—the virtualization collaboration between Microsoft and Citrix. Icento is located in Rotterdam, The Netherlands, and delivers solutions for desktops, unified communications, and virtualization and systems management. Icento delivers state-of-the-art ICT solutions for a broad set of international customers. You can find more information about Icento at www.icento.nl.

Kevin Howell is a highly versatile Strategic Senior Enterprise Architect with demonstrable experience in the government, public, and private market sectors. He has cleared SC with a proven track record of architecting complex infrastructures and developing new reusable service lines, from inception to delivery.

He has over 20 years of professional IT experience. He is a solution architecture with a strong understanding of application of the TOGAF, ITIL, and AGILE frameworks and methodologies.

Kevin is a good communicator with great leadership qualities along with an exceptional ability to adapt and accommodate to changing requirements. He is a positive and optimistic person, committed to maintaining high standards, and is able to cope with increasing demands and pressure.

Kevin is qualified in, and has worked on, enterprise architecture design in the following technologies:

- ▶ VMware
- ▶ Citrix
- ▶ Microsoft
- ▶ Novell
- ▶ Linux
- ▶ ThinPrint
- ▶ Cortado
- ▶ Cisco infrastructure
- ▶ HP Hardware/SAN
- ▶ Cloud services

He is a specialist in Cloud, VMware VCP, VCAP, Citrix CCA, CCEA, CCEE, Microsoft MCSE, Linux, Cisco CCNA, ThinPrint .print Master, Novell Master CNE, TOGAF, Agile, ITIL, and Prince II.

He is the owner of Howell Computing, an IT specialist consulting company with customers such as Fujitsu, British Telecom, DWP, and British Gas.

I would like to thank my wife, Sarah Howell, for her endless support.

www.PacktPub.com

Support files, eBooks, discount offers and more

You might want to visit www.PacktPub.com for support files and downloads related to your book.

Did you know that Packt offers eBook versions of every book published, with PDF and ePub files available? You can upgrade to the eBook version at www.PacktPub.com and, as a print book customer, you are entitled to a discount on the eBook copy. Get in touch with us at service@packtpub.com for more details.

At www.PacktPub.com, you can also read a collection of free technical articles, sign up for a range of free newsletters and receive exclusive discounts and offers on Packt books and eBooks.

http://PacktLib.PacktPub.com

Do you need instant solutions to your IT questions? PacktLib is Packt's online digital book library. Here, you can access, read and search across Packt's entire library of books.

Why Subscribe?

- Fully searchable across every book published by Packt
- Copy and paste, print and bookmark content
- On demand and accessible via web browser

Free Access for Packt account holders

If you have an account with Packt at www.PacktPub.com, you can use this to access PacktLib today and view nine entirely free books. Simply use your login credentials for immediate access.

Table of Contents

Preface

Citrix EdgeSight for XenApp provides the most comprehensive performance-management and reporting solution for the Citrix XenApp infrastructure. Administrators have real-time visibility to session-level performance and provide visibility into key metrics such as profile load time and login script execution.

Citrix EdgeSight is a complicated tool and a beast of an application in itself. With this in mind, we've made an attempt to cover the recipes that a Citrix administrator might come across while managing and supporting their XenApp farm on a daily basis.

This book follows a cookbook style and is packed with simple yet incredibly effective and practical recipes covering the basics to the advanced. All recipes contain step-by-step instructions with screenshots for practical and easy learning.

What this book covers

Installing EdgeSight Server (Intermediate) will describe the prerequisites to install EdgeSight and illustrates its installation.

Installing EdgeSight agents (Simple) will take an in-depth look at the installation of the EdgeSight agent and lists the troubleshooting steps that should be performed if the agent fails to register with the EdgeSight Server.

Configuring the server settings (Intermediate) will present the common server settings that need to be configured after the installation of the EdgeSight Server.

Configuring users, groups, and authentication (Intermediate) will focus on other settings that we should also configure after the installation of the EdgeSight Server.

Defining alerts (Advanced) will explore EdgeSight alerts and illustrate how to create alerts and define action when the defined alert condition is/are met.

Managing the real-time dashboard (Intermediate) will assist in setting up the real-time dashboard to provide a comprehensive view of the XenApp server health state in real time.

Working with EdgeSight reports (Intermediate) will walk through the steps required to work with built-in reports and how to subscribe to reports for automatic delivery.

Monitoring the Citrix license usage (Intermediate) will describe how EdgeSight can be used to report Citrix usage in your environment.

Resolving performance problems (Advanced) will focus on how to use EdgeSight to ensure applications are meeting business metrics at all times by monitoring performance from the user's perspective.

Grooming EdgeSight database (Advanced) will take an in-depth look at how to groom the EdgeSight database to optimize its performance.

What you need for this book

To try out the recipes in this book, you will need to build a Citrix XenApp farm. For the EdgeSight database, you can use the same database server that is being used as the data store for your XenApp farm. Another infrastructure server that is used in the recipes is the messaging server (Microsoft Exchange Server) to send alerts via e-mail.

Who this book is for

This is an ideal book for Citrix XenApp professionals who need to keep a close eye on the performance of their XenApp servers and generate reports.

This cookbook explores basic to advanced recipes that cover the most common tasks a professional might undertake while administering their EdgeSight Server in their day-to-day job.

Conventions

In this book, you will find a number of styles of text that distinguish between different kinds of information. Here are some examples of these styles and an explanation of their meaning.

Code words in text, database table names, folder names, filenames, file extensions, pathnames, dummy URLs, user input, and Twitter handles are shown as follows: "The `EdgeSightXA6Agentx64.msi` installer file is used to install EdgeSight agent Version 5.4, while `EdgeSightXAAgentx64.msi` is used to install EdgeSight agent Version 5.3."

Any command-line input or output is written as follows:

```
Msiexec /i EdgeSightXA6Agentx64.msi /l logfile.log /q SERVER_
NAME=ServerName COMPANY=CompanyName DEPARTMENT=DeptName
REBOOT=ReallySuppress
```

New terms and **important words** are shown in bold. Words that you see on the screen, in menus or dialog boxes for example, appear in the text like this: "Verify that the default departments were created successfully by navigating to **Configure | Company Configuration | Device Management | Departments**."

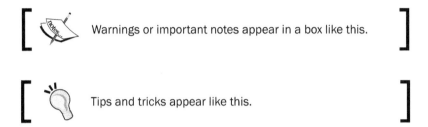

Warnings or important notes appear in a box like this.

Tips and tricks appear like this.

Reader feedback

Feedback from our readers is always welcome. Let us know what you think about this book—what you liked or may have disliked. Reader feedback is important for us to develop titles that you really get the most out of.

To send us general feedback, simply send an e-mail to feedback@packtpub.com, and mention the book title via the subject of your message.

If there is a topic that you have expertise in and you are interested in either writing or contributing to a book, see our author guide on www.packtpub.com/authors.

Customer support

Now that you are the proud owner of a Packt book, we have a number of things to help you to get the most from your purchase.

Errata

Although we have taken every care to ensure the accuracy of our content, mistakes do happen. If you find a mistake in one of our books—maybe a mistake in the text or the code—we would be grateful if you would report this to us. By doing so, you can save other readers from frustration and help us improve subsequent versions of this book. If you find any errata, please report them by visiting http://www.packtpub.com/submit-errata, selecting your book, clicking on the **errata submission form** link, and entering the details of your errata. Once your errata are verified, your submission will be accepted and the errata will be uploaded on our website or added to any list of existing errata, under the Errata section of that title. Any existing errata can be viewed by selecting your title from http://www.packtpub.com/support.

Piracy

Piracy of copyright material on the Internet is an ongoing problem across all media. At Packt, we take the protection of our copyright and licenses very seriously. If you come across any illegal copies of our works, in any form, on the Internet, please provide us with the location address or website name immediately so that we can pursue a remedy.

Please contact us at `copyright@packtpub.com` with a link to the suspected pirated material.

We appreciate your help in protecting our authors, and our ability to bring you valuable content.

Questions

You can contact us at `questions@packtpub.com` if you are having a problem with any aspect of the book, and we will do our best to address it.

Instant EdgeSight for XenApp

Welcome to *Instant EdgeSight for XenApp*. The focus of this book will be on EdgeSight for XenApp, which will include EdgeSight Server, EdgeSight Server Console, EdgeSight agents, the database server, web server, and Citrix License Server.

Installing EdgeSight Server (Intermediate)

We will now perform an installation of Citrix EdgeSight Server 5.4 and also discuss its prerequisites. If possible, you should install the server components on separate servers but they can all be installed together on a single server.

Getting ready

Install the following roles and features using the server manager before proceeding with the installation of the EdgeSight Server in Windows Server 2008:

- Microsoft .NET Framework 3.5 SP1
- Microsoft Message Queuing (MSMQ); install common components only
- IIS 7.0 (also install the following web server roles)
    - Static Content
    - Default Document
    - ASP.NET
    - ISAPI Extensions

- ISAPI Filters
- Windows Authentication
- Request Filtering
- The following management tools:
    - IIS 6 Management Compatibility
    - IIS 6 Metabase Compatibility
    - IIS 6 WMI Compatibility
    - IIS 6 Scripting
    - IIS 6 Management Console

For your database server you can use SQL Server 2008 R2, SQL Server 2008 SP2, or SQL Server 2005 SP4. SQL Server 2012 is the supported database server. Citrix has a database matrix; you can check the article *Citrix Document ID CTX114501* at the following link:

```
http://support.citrix.com/article/CTX114501
```

How to do it...

In this recipe we are going to perform the required operations for installing the EdgeSight Server:

1. Insert the Citrix XenApp CD and click on **Manually install components**.

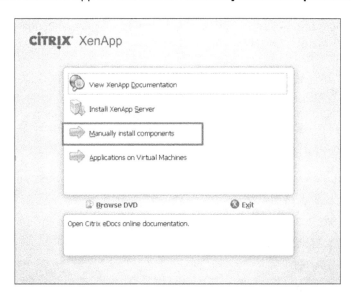

2. Click on **Server Components** and then click on **Application Performance Monitoring**.

3. On the **Welcome** screen, click on **EdgeSight Server** and then click on **Next**.

4. Select **Edgesight Server Website and Database**; click on **Next**.

5. Click on **Warning** to read the warning message, ignore the SSL certificates warning if not using SSL certificates, and click on **OK**.

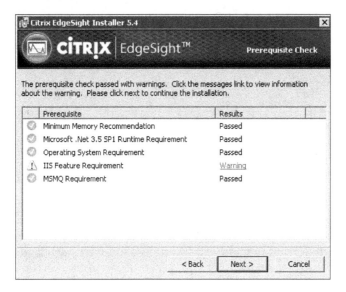

6. Accept the **License Agreement** checkbox and select **Custom** as the setup type.

7. Enter the name of your database server and click on **Test Connect** after selecting the appropriate authentication method.

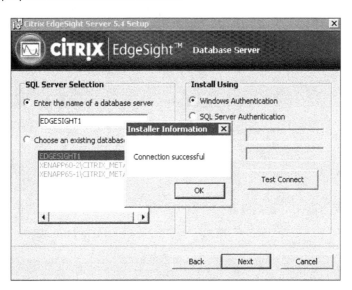

8. Enter the name of the new database that will be created on the database server.

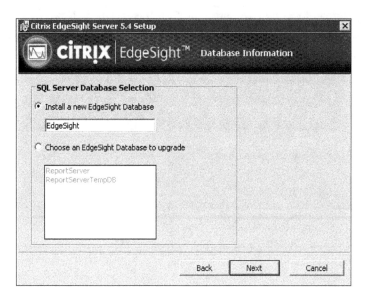

9. Enter the credentials that the web server uses when connecting to the database and then click on **Validate**. After successful validation click on **Next**.

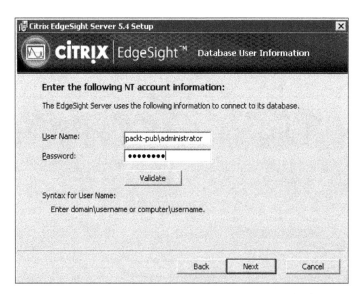

10. Accept the default sizes for the **File Group Size** and **Log Files Size** options and click on **Next**.

11. Accept the default path or modify it if required, click on **Next**, and then on **Install**.

12. Verify that **Go to the EdgeSight Server website now.** is checked and click on **Finish**.

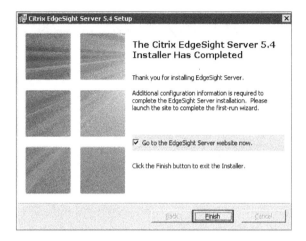

13. Click on **Next** to continue with the **Post Installation Setup Wizard** web page to configure initial configuration of the EdgeSight Server.

 This wizard can also be completed later by going to `http://<ServerName>/edgesight/`

14. Enter a name in the company **Name** field and select the **Time Zone** and **Language** values you want to use for this company. Then click on **Next**.

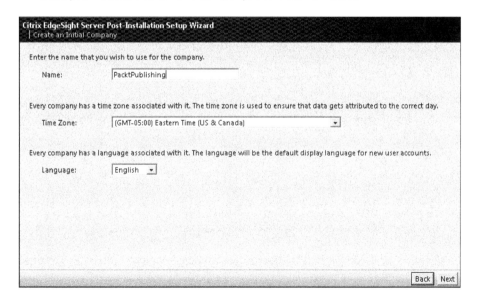

15. Create a Superuser account with a valid e-mail address.

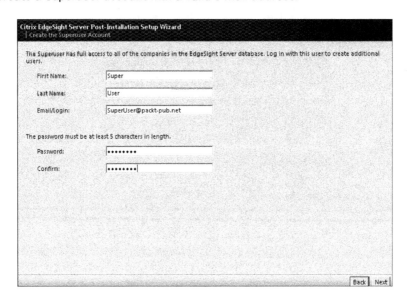

16. Enter the FQDN or IP address of your SMTP server to be used to route the e-mails generated by the EdgeSight Server.

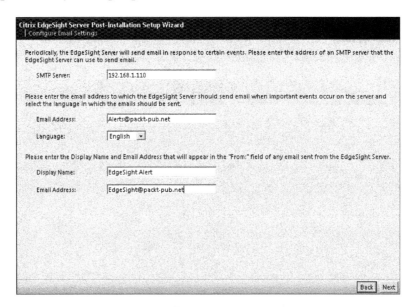

17. Select the type of agents from the drop-down menu for which uploads are supported according to your licenses.

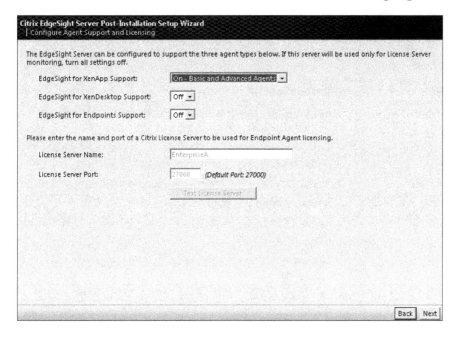

18. Review your choices and click on **Finish**; this will open the EdgeSight Server login web page.

How it works...

The EdgeSight Server is managed through a web-based console and can be accessed from any desktop with Internet Explorer 7.0 or greater with JavaScript enabled. Other software components that are needed on the system from which users access the EdgeSight Server web console include:

► Adobe Flash
► Adobe Reader
► Microsoft Excel

To update the Excel spreadsheets, EdgeSight requires full write permissions; therefore you should use the Microsoft Excel that comes with Microsoft Office 2003 or 2007 and not Excel Viewer. Also make sure that you confirm to your Microsoft Office license agreements.

As of this date, Microsoft Excel 2010 is not supported.

There's more...

It is nice to know some EdgeSight terminology; refer to the following table:

Term	Description
Company	Primary organizational unit, a single server can support multiple companies.
Department	Companies are broken into departments and create a hierarchical tree.
Devices	Any system with the EdgeSight agent installed.
Custom Groups	A user-defined collection of devices.
Users	Users who can log in and display reports and perform other administrative tasks.
Superuser	Has access to all companies hosted on the server and can create other users.

A single EdgeSight Server can support multiple companies, each company with its own time zone, SMTP settings, license server, and Superuser account.

The Superuser credential information should be stored and saved for future reference. The Superuser account cannot be deleted.

EdgeSight 5.4 also requires a Citrix License Server 11.6 or above. Without configuring the Citrix License Server, the EdgeSight agents will not upload data to the EdgeSight Server. To monitor your Citrix licensing server, the version of the licensing server should be at least 11.9.

If you plan to install License Administration Console and EdgeSight Server on the same machine then install EdgeSight Server first.

Only Enterprise and Platinum licenses are supported to be used by EdgeSight 5.4.

 Enterprise licenses monitor only the basic metrics.

Installing EdgeSight agents (Simple)

The EdgeSight agent needs to be installed on each XenApp server that we need to monitor. After the agent has been installed, the agent attempts to contact the EdgeSight Server to download its configuration. The installation of the agent requires a reboot of the server and may take up to 10 minutes before the XenApp server appears in the EdgeSight Console.

Getting ready

If you have to use a proxy server, remember that, for the communication to happen between the EdgeSight agent and the server, you must configure a proxy to route the EdgeSight traffic to the EdgeSight Server. You can do this by reconfiguring the EdgeSight agent network settings of the Citrix System Monitoring Agent with these new proxy values.

The following screenshot shows the EdgeSight agent settings screen where you need to provide the proxy settings:

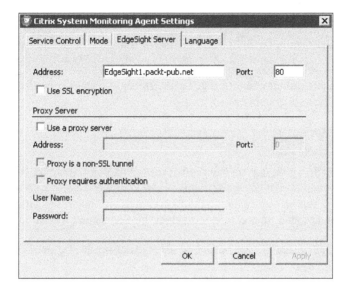

You must also configure antivirus software running on your EdgeSight Server and all XenApp servers with EdgeSight agent to exclude specific processes and files.

Antivirus exclusions

Ensure that these agent services are not subject to script blocking on both the EdgeSight Server and the XenApp server.

EdgeSight Server	XenApp Server
RSshApp.exe	RScorsvc.exe
RSshSvc.exe	

These files are located in the following folders:

▶ The RSshApp.exe and RSshSvc.exe files are located at %CommonProgramFiles%\Citrix\System Monitoring\ Server\RSSH\

  ▶ The `RScorsvc.exe` file is located at `%ProgramFiles%\Citrix\System Monitoring\Agent\Core\`

Also exclude the following folders from script blocking:

EdgeSight Server	XenApp Server
`%ProgramFiles%\Citrix\System Monitoring\Server`	`%ALLUSERSPROFILE%\Citrix\System Monitoring\Data`
`%ProgramFiles%\Microsoft SQL Server\MSSQL\Data\`	
`%SystemRoot%\SYSTEM32\Logfiles`	

For XenApp servers with Windows Server 2003 the `%ALLUSERSPROFILE%\Citrix\System Monitoring\Data` folder can be found at `%ALLUSERSPROFILE%\Application Data\Citrix\System Monitoring\Data\`

How to do it...

1. The EdgeSight agent can be installed during the XenApp installation or after the XenApp installation. If you want to install the EdgeSight agent with the installation of the XenApp server, during the installation of the XenApp server, when selecting the roles to be installed, make sure you select the **EdgeSight Agent** option:

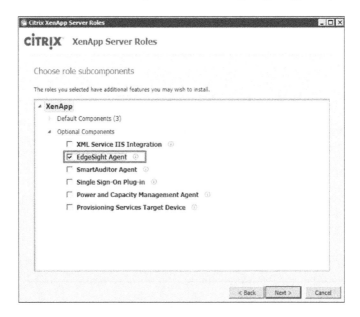

2. The EdgeSight agent can also be installed after the installation of XenApp or on an existing XenApp server. The XenApp 6.5 CD image contains two agent installer files, as shown in the following screenshot:

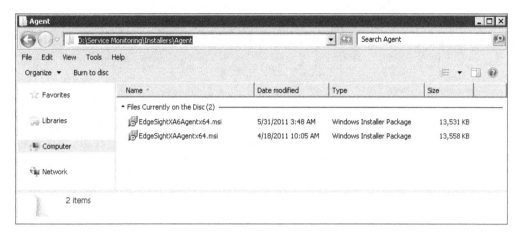

The `EdgeSightXA6Agentx64.msi` installer file is used to install EdgeSight agent Version 5.4, while `EdgeSightXAAgentx64.msi` is used to install EdgeSight agent Version 5.3.

The installation of the agent is straightforward; the only thing one should keep in mind is that the company name should match the name specified during the EdgeSight Server setup.

3. The agent can also be installed via the command-line interface. A typical command line to install the agent would be:

```
Msiexec /i EdgeSightXA6Agentx64.msi /l logfile.log /q SERVER_
NAME=ServerName COMPANY=CompanyName DEPARTMENT=DeptName
REBOOT=ReallySuppress
```

How it works...

The agent runs as a service and collects the data from a number of sources including Windows Management Instrumentation (WMI) and Windows Performance Counters.

The XenApp agent collects performance data every 15 seconds and periodically consolidates this data into five-minute samples. The data uploaded to the EdgeSight Server is consolidated into an hourly granularity. By default, this data is uploaded to the EdgeSight Server once a day.

There's more...

If you ever need to modify the agent configuration after installation, you can use the **Citrix System Monitoring Agent** control panel applet on the XenApp server.

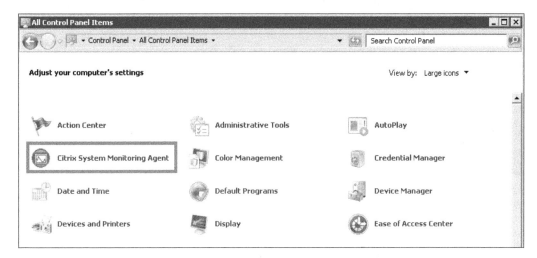

The EdgeSight agent operates in either the basic mode or the advanced mode. The agents in advanced mode collect more detailed metrics. For more details on the differences, refer to the *Citrix Document ID CTX124427* documentation at `http://support.citrix.com/article/CTX124427`.

XenApp Edition	Default Agent Mode	Mode Tab Availability
Platinum	Advanced	No
Enterprise	Basic	Yes

To configure the agent mode when installing the agent using the command line, add the `FUNCTIONALITY_MODE` argument. It can have two values `Advanced` and `Basic`.

Configuring the server settings (Intermediate)

Now that the installation and the post-installation wizards have completed successfully, we still need to complete a few tasks such as configuring the Reporting Services, creating departments, and groups.

Getting ready

Reporting Services is a component of Microsoft SQL Server and is required as part of a Citrix EdgeSight installation to provide a robust and flexible reporting environment. Reporting Services provides a central location for report storage and management. They can be installed on the database server, web server, or a separate server itself. If you do not have Reporting Services configured, the EdgeSight installation process will not give any warning; the installation will end successfully but no reports will be available on the EdgeSight Console.

You can open a web browser and point the URL to `http://<ServerName>/ReportServer` to verify the existence of Reporting Services on a server. This URL could be different if the Reporting Services were customized. This is depicted in the following screenshot:

This web page also displays the version of the Reporting Services we have installed.

For more information on how to install and configure Reporting Services to be used by EdgeSight, refer to the *Citrix Article ID CTX111313* documentation at the following link:

`http://support.citrix.com/article/CTX111313`

How to do it...

1. As soon as you log in for the first time on the EdgeSight web console, you will see a message on the top such as **Reporting Services is not configured or is configured incorrectly**. In the **Report Server URL** field, enter the URL of your reporting server and the credentials for the Reporting Server. Click on the **Save Changes** button.

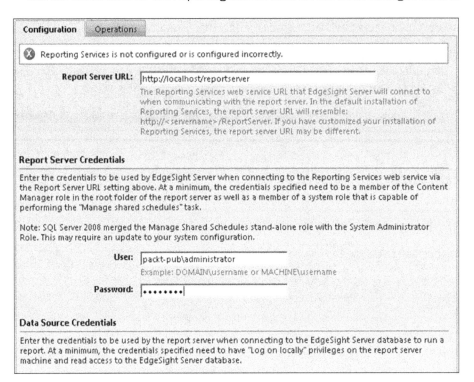

If you have created a new user ID to be used by the EdgeSight Server to connect Reporting Services web services, use this ID. You can later modify the information entered here by navigating to **Configure | Server Configuration | Reporting Services | Report Server**.

2. The **Reporting Services Configuration Status – Webpage Dialog** window pops up. Wait a few minutes for the pop-up window to configure the Reporting Services. Once the Reporting Services have been configured, click on the **Close** button.

 A department is a logical grouping of agent devices within a company that have the same configurations and alerts applied. We can map one or multiple alert rules, alert actions, worker configurations, and agent configurations to devices in the department.

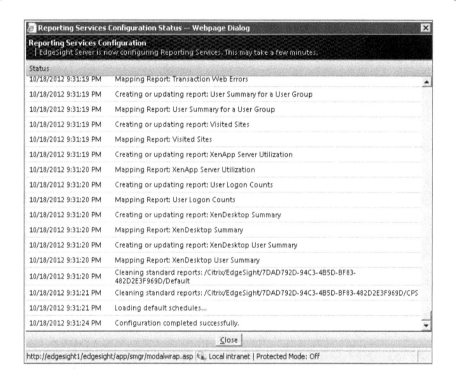

If the **Reporting Services Configuration Status – Webpage Dialog** window does not appear and times out after 20 minutes, there is a delay in communication from the EdgeSight web server with SQL Server Reporting Services. If this happens then ensure that the SQL Server Agent service is in *started* state. This is required for publishing the schedules.

3. Verify that the default departments were created successfully by navigating to **Configure | Company Configuration | Device Management | Departments**.

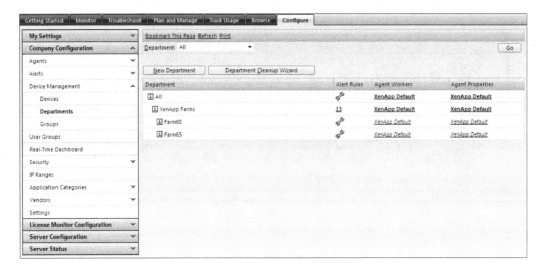

The **All** root department and the **XenApp Farms** subdepartments are created by default during the EdgeSight installation and are usually referred as the default departments. The default departments cannot be renamed, moved, or deleted but we can modify their worker and agent properties.

The subdepartments override configuration settings inherited from parent departments. If you have two alerts mapped to the **All** department and three are mapped to a subdepartment, then that means that a total of five alert rules will be applied to this subdepartment.

You can create departments based on the type of application published on the XenApp server such as the Office 2007 servers, the Office 2010 servers, the geographical location of the server, or any other hierarchical structure.

4. After installing the EdgeSight agent and rebooting the XenApp server you will receive an e-mail from the EdgeSight Server that a new instance has been discovered. Verify that you start getting those e-mails. The following screenshot displays the e-mail received from the EdgeSight Server after a new device gets registered with it:

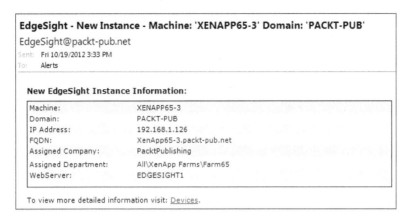

5. Navigate to **Configure | Company Configuration | Device Management | Devices** to verify that the XenApp servers on which the agent has been installed start to appear in the EdgeSight console.

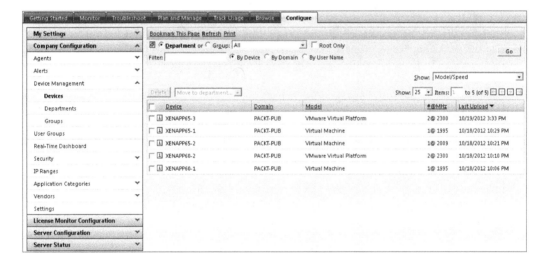

6. Verify the EdgeSight Server's license status by navigating to **Configure | Server Configuration | EdgeSight Licensing**.

> If a XenApp agent licensing violation has occurred, then the following message will be displayed:
>
> **EdgeSight has detected a problem with Licensing. Click here for more information.**

7. Verify that you only upload the data from the agents to the EdgeSight database that is important to you. Navigate to **Configure | Server Configuration | Data Maintenance | Upload Configuration** to make your selection according to your requirements.

An important message is displayed at the top of the page, informing the administrator that the amount of data uploaded to the server directly impacts the size of your database and the performance of the server. The server will run faster and will be able to support more devices if you do not upload data that is not important to you.

There's more...

A single server can support multiple companies. Companies are broken down into departments.

To display the most recent messages related to server maintenance jobs, events, or the registration of new agents, browse to **Server Status | Messages**.

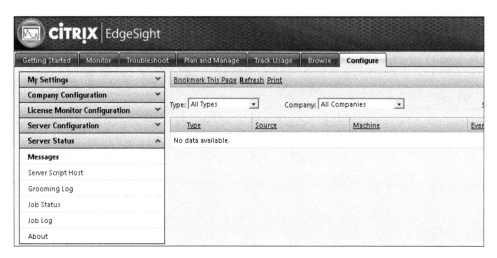

Modifying the e-mail notification settings

You must provide a valid SMTP server name or IP address as the EdgeSight Server uses e-mail for alerts and error event notifications.

In case you ever need to go back and modify the e-mail notification settings for a company in EdgeSight, navigate to **Configure | Server Configuration | Settings | Notifications**.

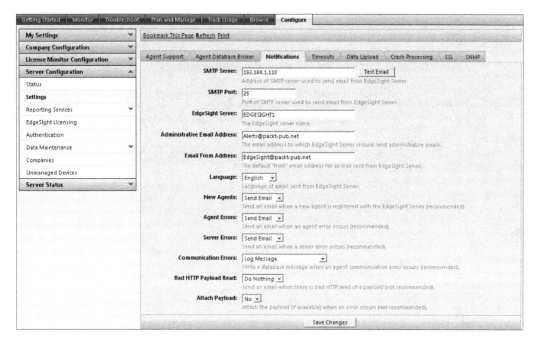

Before saving your changes you must also test the communication with your messaging server by clicking on the **Test Email** button.

Based on your SMTP server and its version, you might also need to configure you SMTP server to allow the EdgeSight Server to send an e-mail.

Configuring users, groups, and authentication (Intermediate)

After you've completed the EdgeSight Server installation and configured the server setting, it is time to create users, assign groups, and configure an authentication provider. In this recipe we will use Active Directory as the authentication provider.

Getting ready

Before creating a new Active Directory as the authentication provider we need to get the LDAP path. The LDAP path is formulated as LDAP://DomainName.com.

How to do it...

1. To configure an authentication provider, browse to **Configure | Server Configuration | Authentication** and click on the **New Provider** button.

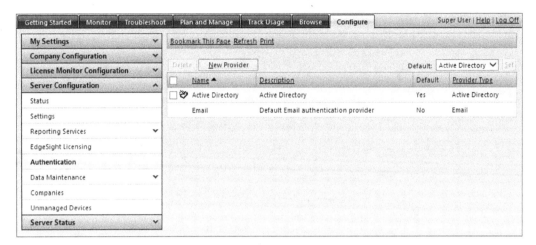

 The default authentication provider that is created with the installation of EdgeSight cannot be edited or deleted.

2. Select **Active Directory** from the list of authentication provider and click on **Next**.

3. Enter a name and description to identify the provider. If you want to configure this as the default authentication provider then also select **Make this the default authentication provider**. Also enter the LDAP path with the appropriate user credentials and then click on the **Test** button. After the message **The test completed successfully**, click on the **Finish** button.

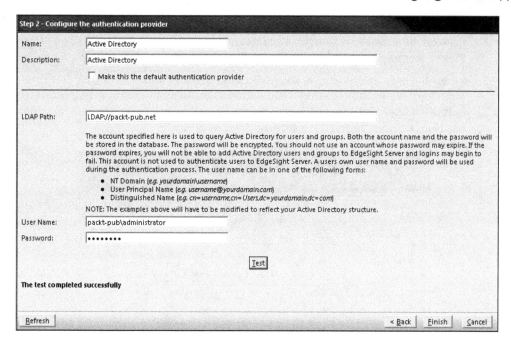

4. Now we will create a new user in EdgeSight using the Active Directory User Picker and select a user from our Active Directory domain. To do this navigate to **Configure | Company Configuration | Security | Users** and then click on the **New User** button.

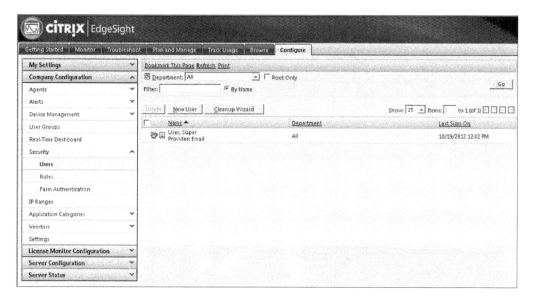

5. Select **Active Directory** as the authentication provider and click on **Next**.

6. Click on the **Browse** button to select **User** or **Group** from the **Active Directory User Picker** window.

7. Select the appropriate type as **Users**, **Groups**, or **Users and Groups** from the **Type** drop-down menu and click on the **Go** button to populate the list from Active Directory. Select the **User** or **Group** value you want to assign the permissions to and click on **OK**. Here we have selected the **Domain Admins** group.

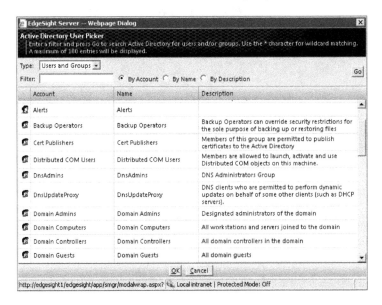

8. Click on the **Save** button to select the role from the **Role Picker** pop-up window.

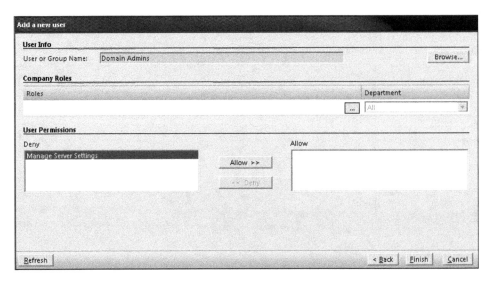

9. Select the role you want to make this new user a member of and click on **OK**. You will be then returned to the **Add a new user** web page.

10. Select user permissions to be granted to the user from the **Deny** list box and click on **Allow** to grant the permission.

11. Click on **Finish** and verify that the new user you created now appears in the list.

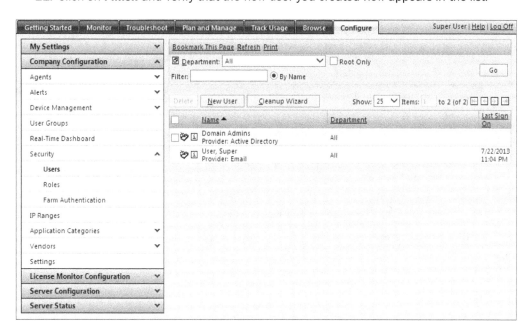

Let us now see how to manage groups.

The **User Groups** page enables you to create collections of users by directly selecting users by username, IP address, IP range, or by running a query against the EdgeSight database. The examples of groups include common operating systems and common hardware:

1. To create a group, browse to **Configure | Company Configuration | Device Management | Groups** and then click on the **New Group** button.

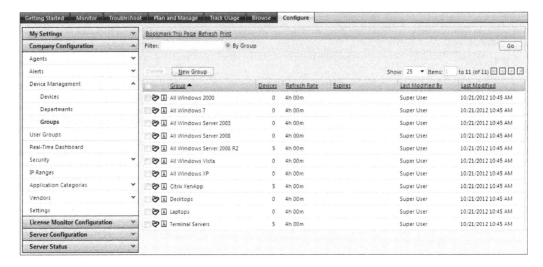

The groups in the previous screenshot were created automatically during the installation of the EdgeSight Server.

2. Enter a name for the group and click on the **Create a Group** button.

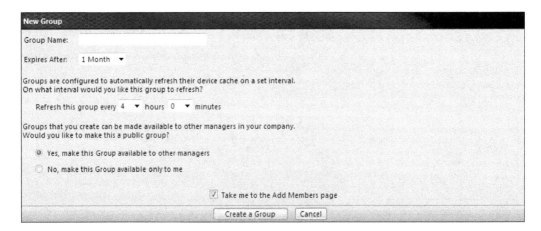

The expiration period is the time after which this newly created group will automatically be deleted. This feature facilitates the management of groups created for short-term projects with a set duration, such as the evaluation of software. Groups can also be set to never expire.

The refresh period refreshes the device cache. This refresh rate generally provides you with sufficient currency of data without performing unnecessary cache refreshes.

How it works...

If you do not create the Active Directory authentication provider, you can still use the default authentication provider (**Email**) that is installed with the installation of the EdgeSight Server. The default authentication provider uses an e-mail address as the username:

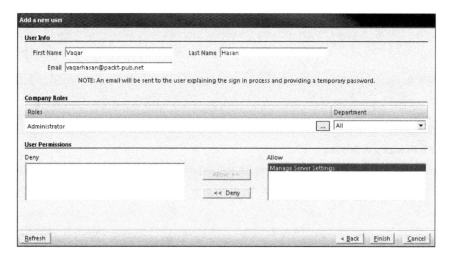

When you create a new user, you will have to provide the e-mail address for that user. Then an e-mail is send to the user explaining the first-time login process and also providing a temporary password. When the user first logs in, they are requested to change their password.

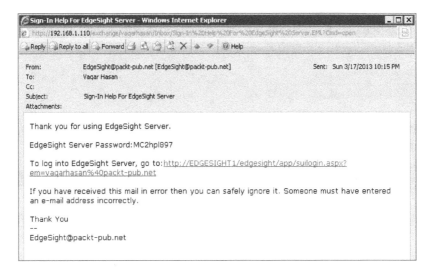

Once you have configured Active Directory as the authentication provider, then the users or groups you assigned the permissions will be able to log in to the EdgeSight website using their Active Directory credentials.

Defining alerts (Advanced)

Citrix EdgeSight alert is a powerful rules- and actions-based system that instructs the EdgeSight agents to send an alert in real time when a predefined situation has occurred on a monitored object. Alerts are defined by rules.

The action can be configured to send either an e-mail alert or SNMP trap. The generated alerts are also listed and organized within the EdgeSight web console.

After an alert rule has been created, it should be mapped to a department.

How to do it...

1. To create an alert, navigate to **Configure | Company Configuration | Alerts | Rules | New Alert Rule**.

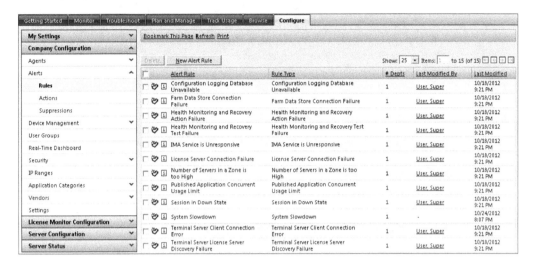

2. We will create an alert rule based on an application, so select the **Application Alerts** radio button and click on **Next**.

3. Select **Application Performance** as the alert type and click on **Next**.

4. Give the alert rule a name, the name of the process we want to monitor, and the CPU time in percent. Click on **Next**.

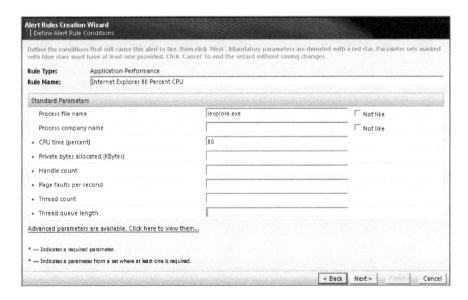

5. Select departments to assign this alert rule to and click on **Next**.

6. Select the department you wish to edit alert actions in and click on **Next**.

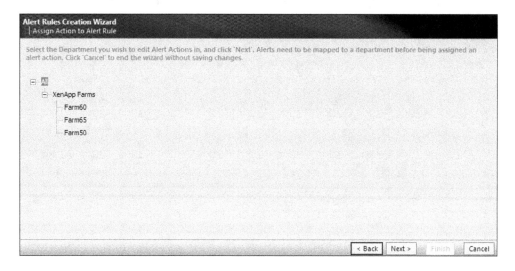

7. We now need to assign an action to this alert rule; we will create a new action. So select the **Create New Alert Action** radio button and click on **Next**.

8. We will send an e-mail notification as the alert action so select **Send an email notification** radio button and click on **Next**.

9. Enter a name, subject, and one or more recipient e-mail addresses for this e-mail action. You can click the **Test Action** button to test whether EdgeSight was able to successfully queue the message or not. Click on **Finish**.

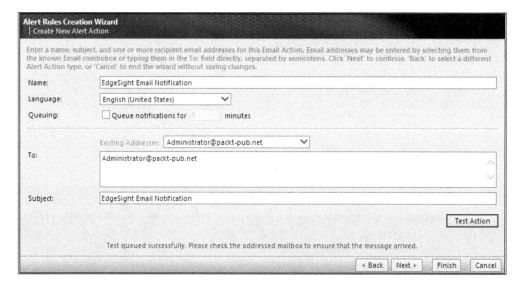

How it works...

Creating too many real-time alerts can affect the XenApp server performance as each rule that is created requires more work to be performed by the agent.

We should only create alerts for those critical situations that require immediate action. If the situation is not critical, the delivery of alerts based on the normal upload cycle will probably be sufficient.

By default, the alert data and other statistics are uploaded to the server daily.

There's more...

When a new alert rule is created or any existing rule is modified, this change is applied to all the devices in the department when those devices next upload data to the EdgeSight Server; alternatively, you can manually upload the alert rule data by clicking on **Run Remotely**.

Administrators can also force certain agent devices to perform a configuration check within the EdgeSight web console by navigating to **Configure** | **Company Configuration** | **Agents** and then selecting the device from the device picker.

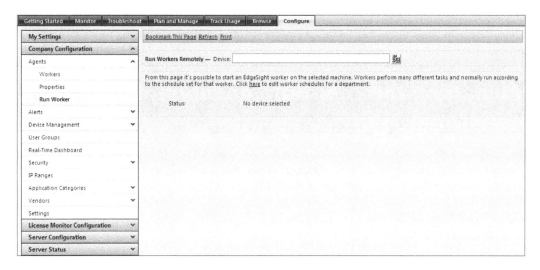

We can also temporarily prevent certain types of alert that match a criterion from being displayed on the console using **Alert Suppression**.

To suppress an alert, navigate to **Monitor | Alert List**, click on the down arrow ⏷, and then select **Suppress Alert**.

To clear an alert navigate to **Configure | Company Configuration | Alerts | Suppressions**.

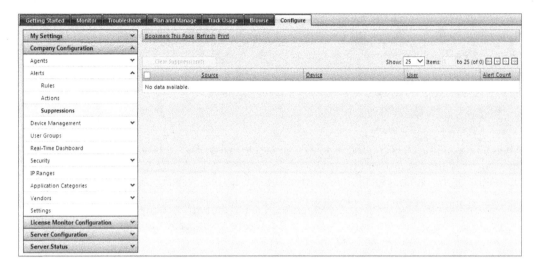

This is per user basis and other EdgeSight administrators will still see those alerts suppressed by you.

Managing the real-time dashboard (Intermediate)

The EdgeSight dashboard provides a comprehensive view of the XenApp server's health state in real time. The dashboard queries the agent databases for counter values based on the configuration created by the EdgeSight administrator.

Getting ready

To populate the dashboard, we first need to create a new real-time configuration. Each configuration defines what counters will be displayed in the dashboard. We can create multiple configurations and each configuration will have its own devices. A device can be a member of multiple configurations.

How to do it...

1. Log on to the EdgeSight website, navigate to **Configure | Company Configuration | Real-Time Dashboard**, and then click on the **New Real Time Configuration** button.

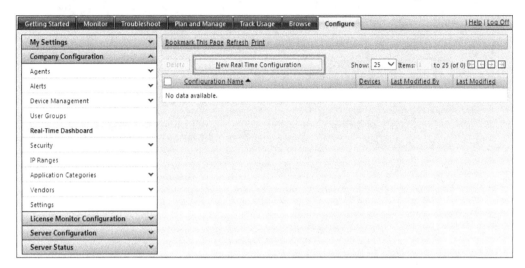

2. Enter a name for the configuration, verify **that Take me to the Add Devices and Counter wizard** is checked, and then click on **the Create the Configuration** button.

3. This takes us to the **Edit Devices** screen. To populate the list, click on **Go** button and then double-click on the device name to add it to the **Configuration Members** list. Click on **Next**.

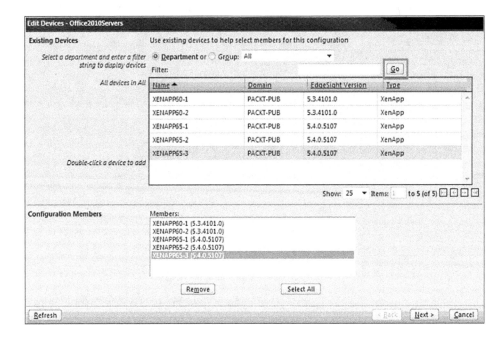

 Each configuration can contain a maximum of 20 devices and each configuration can only monitor a maximum of 8 counters.

4. Checkmark the counter that you want to monitor and enter the threshold value for that counter. Click on **Next** and then click on **Finish**.

Edit Counters - Office2010Servers

Performance Counters	Threshold			Threshold	
CPU					
☑ % Privileged Time	40	%	☐ % Total Processor Time	40	%
☐ % User Time	40	%	☐ Interrupts per Second	1000	/sec
☐ Privileged Time secs	10	second(s)	☐ Processor Time secs	10	second(s)
☐ User Time secs	10	second(s)			
Memory					
☑ % Committed Bytes In Use	40	%	☐ Committed Kbytes	1024000	KB
☐ Page Faults per Second	1000	/sec	☐ Pages Input per Second	10	/sec
☐ Pool NonPaged KBytes	64000	KB	☐ Pool Paged KBytes	256000	KB
TCP					
☑ Current Connections	30	connection(s)	☐ Failed Connections	30	connection(s)
☐ Reset Connections	10	connection(s)	☐ Segments Received per Second	100	/sec
☐ Segments Retransmitted	10	/sec	☐ Segments Sent per Second	100	/sec
Disk					
☑ % Disk Time	40	%	☐ Current Disk Queue Length	2	request(s)
☐ Disk Kbytes per Second	50	KB / sec			
System					
☑ Context Switches per Second	10000	/sec	☐ Process Count	60	process(es)
☐ Processor Queue Length	5	thread(s)	☐ System Calls per Second	20000	/sec

XenApp Counters	Threshold			Threshold	
Session Counts					
☑ Active Sessions	40	session(s)	☐ Inactive Sessions	20	session(s)
☐ Total Sessions	40	session(s)			
EUEM Counters					
☑ Average ICA Round Trip Time	100	ms	☐ Average Network Round Trip Time	100	ms
☐ Peak ICA Round Trip Time	100	ms	☐ Peak Network Round Trip Time	100	ms

| Refresh | | < Back | Next > | Cancel |

5. Click on the name of the configuration you just created. In this case it is **Office2010Servers**.

6. Click on **Start Updating**. To stop querying the devices, click on **Stop Updating**.

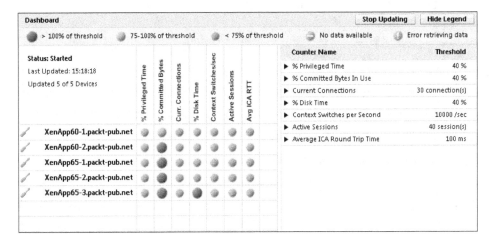

There's more...

If the threshold for a device consistently exceeds your defined threshold, you may use the device troubleshooter icon to further investigate the root cause of the problem.

Working with EdgeSight reports (Intermediate)

EdgeSight reports are based on the data stored in the agent database as well as the server database. The reports can be historical as well as real-time. In case of real-time reports, the data is pulled directly from the agent database.

In this recipe we will subscribe to a report and configure it to be delivered via an e-mail.

Getting ready

EdgeSight comes with a wide range of built-in reports. We can download these reports and/or export them to a variety of different formats. We can also add our own custom reports to the report server. One great feature that EdgeSight also offers is the automatic delivery of the report of our choice to run at a custom schedule; the report is sent to a specific folder or e-mail addresses.

How to do it...

1. First we need to verify that the e-mail settings for the Reporting Services are configured properly. Log on to the server hosting your reporting services, open the **Reporting Services Configuration Manager**, and then select **Email Settings**. By default the **Sender Address** and **SMTP Server** fields are not populated automatically. After entering the appropriate information click on **Apply**.

 The **Sender Address** field should be a valid e-mail address and appears as the address of origin in the e-mail.

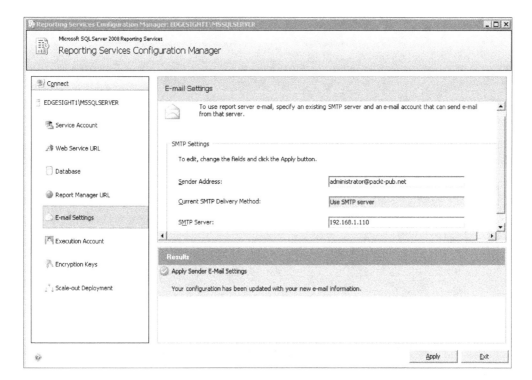

 Ensure that SMTP relaying is permitted by your mail server and that it also allows the EdgeSight Server to relay mail; otherwise, the recipients will not receive e-mails from the EdgeSight Server.

2. Open the EdgeSight website, navigate to **Configure** | **Server Configuration** | **Reporting Services** | **Schedules**, and then click on the **New Schedule** button.

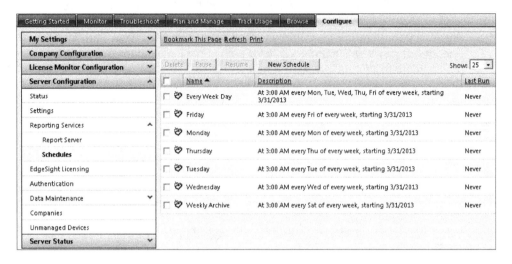

3. Specify a name for the schedule and specify other details as per your requirement. Click on the **Add Schedule** button.

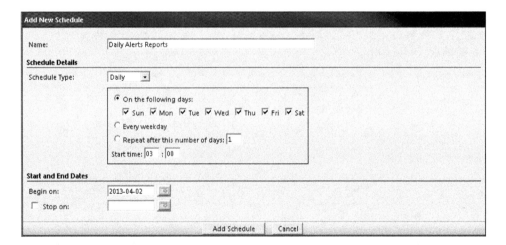

 The start time is based on a 24-hour clock.

4. Click on the **Browse** tab and the **Subscriptions** link of the report you want to subscribe to.

5. Click on the **New Subscription** button to create a new subscription.

6. The default delivery is through e-mail; in case you want to save the report to a specified folder, you can click on the **Delivered by** drop-down menu and select **File Share**. To select the schedule, click on the **Schedule** drop-down menu and select the schedule you want the report to be processed at; click on the **Create Subscription** button.

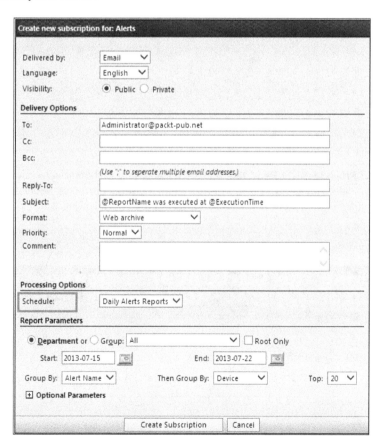

There's more...

The built-in reports provided by EdgeSight can be modified to meet the business requirements more closely. To modify a report, click on the **Download** link and save the file with the default extension of .RDL (Report Definition Language). Then use your favorite XML Editor to open the .RDL file and change the SQL query within the <CommandText> tag. You might also need to modify the field names <Field Name> and the data fields <DataField> tags. Once done save the file, navigate to **Configure | My Settings | Custom Reports**, and then click on the **Upload** button.

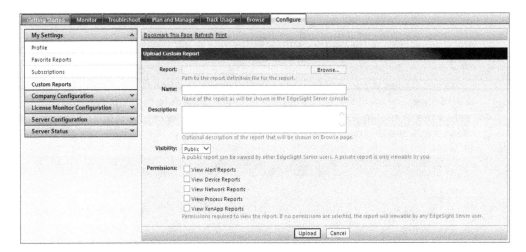

If you set the visibility to **Private**, then only the user uploading the report can view it.

Citrix EdgeSight Reporting wiki is a collaborative authoring web encyclopedia project that has several reports with real-life scenarios and other helpful EdgeSight product information. It is available at the following link:

http://community.citrix.com/edgesight/

Monitoring the Citrix license usage (Intermediate)

EdgeSight can report the usage reported by the Citrix License Server for all types of Citrix licenses used in the organization.

In addition to Citrix licensing, EdgeSight can also display published application usage and session durations with both summary and detailed information. These reports are also available from the **Browse** tab.

Getting ready

To monitor your Citrix licensing server, the version of the licensing server should be at least 11.9.

How to do it...

1. We must first specify at least one Citrix License Server by navigating to **Configure | License Monitor Configuration | License Servers** and then clicking on the **New License Server** button. For the license server name we can specify either the IP address or the FQDN of the license server.

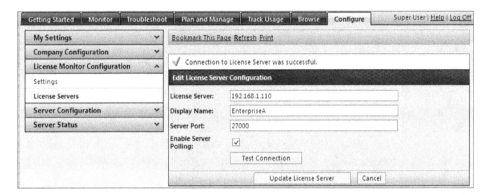

2. To configure the polling interval between two pools, navigate to **Configure | License Monitor Configuration | Settings**.

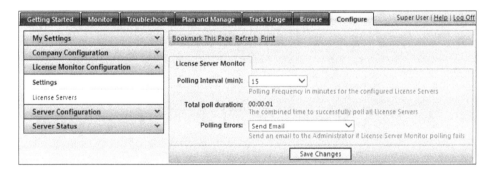

Setting the polling interval to 15 minutes means that a polling cycle will be initiated 15 minutes from the time that the last polling cycle completed.

The total poll duration is the sum of the time taken to successfully poll all the enabled license servers during the last poll. We can use this value to help us set a realistic polling interval.

3. For usage information about the published application, make sure that the **EdgeSight for XenApp Support** feature is configured as **On - Basic and Advanced Agents** by navigating to **Configure | Server Configuration | Settings | Agent Support**.

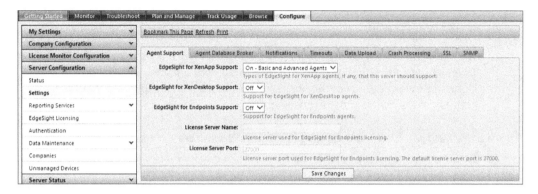

4. To track the usage of Citrix licenses, applications, and session durations, click on the **Track Usage** tab.

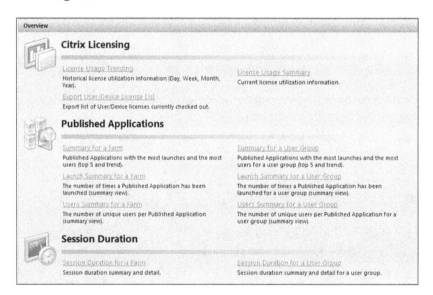

How it works...

Once the license server has been configured for monitoring, EdgeSight Server directly polls the license server for information on license usage.

License server monitoring does not require an EdgeSight agent on the Citrix License Server.

There's more...

To view the license server poller logfile, navigate to **Configure | Server Status | Server Script Host**. Locate the `core_lsm_license_poller` script, then click on the drop-down menu, and select **View Log**.

If there is any error in the polling, the logfile will display the error code and the reason for the failure and an e-mail are also sent to the EdgeSight administrator. If the license server poller is not able to connect to the Citrix License Server then an error code of -96 is written to the logfile.

You can also disable polling on any particular license server for maintenance or any other reason. If you disable polling, the previously collected license information from disabled servers will still appear in the **License Usage Trending** report, but no new license information is displayed for the disabled server in the **License Usage Summary** report until polling is enabled back.

You can also remove a license server configuration from the EdgeSight database by deleting it. If you delete a license server configuration, all license usage data associated with that license server is deleted from the EdgeSight database. After deletion, no data from the license server is displayed in the license usage reports.

Resolving performance problems (Advanced)

EdgeSight provides a centralized console to investigate problems related to sessions, applications, systems, and networks without requiring us to somehow log in or connect to the device having the problem.

Getting ready

The important thing here is that the end device you are troubleshooting should have the EdgeSight agent installed.

How to do it...

1. To get the real-time performance data of a device, navigate to **Troubleshoot | Device Troubleshooter**.

2. Either enter the IP address or the name of the device you are troubleshooting in the **Search** field or browse in the department tree.

    You can also use the slider to change the time frame for the data you want to be displayed.

3. Click on the **Go** button.

4. Click on the **System Summary** tab and look for important counters here such as **Committed Bytes In Use**, which displays the usage of the system memory.

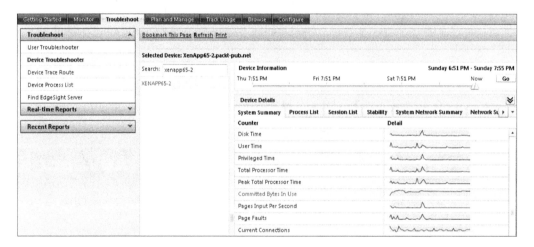

5. Click on the counter you want to have a much deeper look at and EdgeSight will display more detailed information in a pop-up window. You can also click on a point on the pop-up chart to display point-in-time data for the counter.

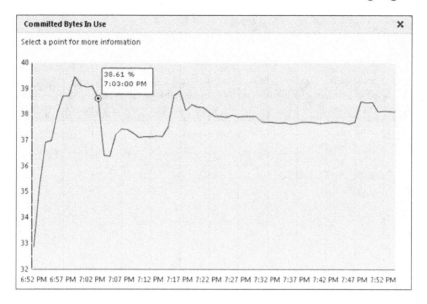

How it works...

In cases where the device is a XenApp server running a basic-level agent, data will not be displayed in some of the tabs; instead, a message is displayed in each affected tab.

There's more...

Similar to **Device Troubleshooter**, the **User Troubleshooter** page can be used to display detailed performance data for sessions across a farm for any specified user. You will need to provide the username, and optionally the name of the server hosting the session, and then click on **Find Sessions**.

Several steps are involved from the time a user clicks on the icon of a published application to launch and use the application till the time the application finally launches. EdgeSight for XenApp can be used to diagnose those slow logins or slow sessions problems reported by the users; it lets you examine the steps involved and the time required to complete each step.

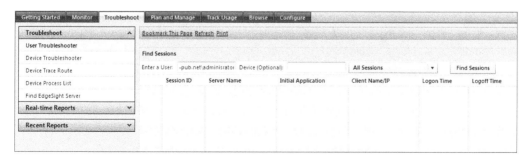

If no default credentials were specified for the farm before, then you can click on the browse button ⌷ and provide the credentials in the **Find a XenApp Session – Webpage Dialog** window.

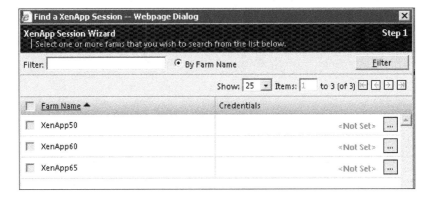

You can specify unique credentials for each XenApp farm in your environment.

You can also use the **Device Process List** page to display detailed information about processes that are currently running on the selected device.

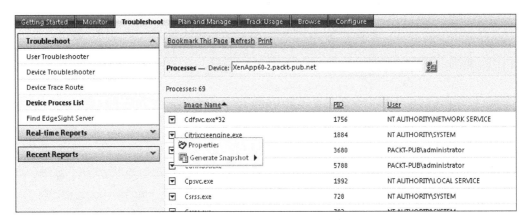

You can also generate a diagnostic snapshot (**Normal** or **Full**), which allows us to remotely analyze the current state of the selected device and investigate whether a particular process is the cause of the problem you are investigating. The snapshot generates a dump file on the selected device and is also uploaded to the server as an alert.

One other very useful troubleshooting tool here is the **Device Trace Route** tool.

The **Device Trace Route** tool can be used to identify and route problems you may have; it allows you to execute a trace route from the selected remote device to a specified network host.

Grooming EdgeSight databases (Advanced)

Due to the large amount of data collected by EdgeSight, it is recommended that good housekeeping should be completed by the EdgeSight administrator for EdgeSight to provide optimal results.

Similar problems can also be noticed if there is not enough disk space on the drive or other problems with the database. As a result of any of these problems, grooming errors might occur and those will also be displayed in the console.

In EdgeSight the primary database management mechanism is called **grooming** and is defined as the process of removing older data from a database at regular intervals to make room for new data.

How to do it...

There are eight data files in the EdgeSight database; the default location of these files is at `C:\Program Files\Microsoft SQL Server\MSSQL10.MSSQLSERVER\MSSQL\DATA\`.

1. We first need to find the data files that are larger in size than other data files. We can run the following query to extract this information:

    ```
    SELECT Name, (size*8)/1024 Size
    FROM sys.master_files
    WHERE DB_NAME(database_id) = 'Edgesight'
    ```

The following table is the output I received after executing the query. Your output (size) will be different:

Name	Size
Edgesight	2,500
Edgesight_log	45,052
Edgesight_FG1_Data	12,820
Edgesight_FG2_Data	25,350
Edgesight_FG3_Data	7,322
Edgesight_FG4_Data	46,623
Edgesight_FG5_Data	8,250
Edgesight_FG6_Data	245,020
Edgesight_FG7_Data	12,500

From the previous results we can see that in our case the database `Edgesight_FG6_Data` is the largest in size. The size is in MBs.

2. The next step is to determine the names of the tables that are hosted by that particular file group. We can determine those names by running the following query:

```
SELECT  DISTINCT object_name(sys.sysindexes.id) as 'Table Name'
,sys.filegroups.name as 'File Group Name'
FROM sys.sysindexes, sys.filegroups
WHERE objectproperty(sys.sysindexes.id,'IsUserTable') = 1
AND sys.filegroups.data_space_id = sys.sysindexes.groupid
ORDER BY sys.filegroups.name
```

The output from this query in my case was as follows:

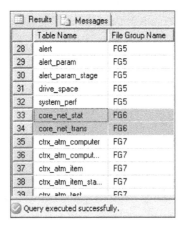

3. The next step now would be to find out the number of rows in each table. Run the following query in SQL Server Management Studio to find the number of rows in both the `core_net_trans` and `core_net_stat` tables:

```
SELECT sysobjects.Name, sysindexes.Rows
FROM sysobjects INNER JOIN sysindexes ON sysobjects.id =
sysindexes.id
WHERE sysindexes.IndId < 2 AND sysobjects.Name IN('core_net_stat',
'core_net_trans')
```

The output from this query in my case was as follows:

Name	Rows
core_net_stat	250475223
core_net_trans	2457843

These results clearly tell us that the table named `core_net_trans` has more rows than `core_net_stat` and hence `core_net_trans` would also be much larger in size compared to `core_net_stat`.

4. The next step would be to find out the number of records that for some reason could not be deleted after the number of Groom Days has passed. The default **Groom Days** value for both the `core_net_trans` and `core_net_stat` tables is 10 days. To verify the Groom Days you can navigate to **Configure | Server Configuration | Data Maintenance | Grooming**.

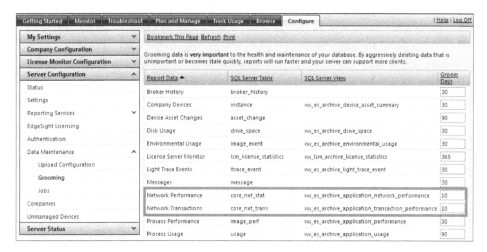

5. We can use the following query to determine the number of records (if any) that could not be deleted:

```
SELECT COUNT(*) FROM CORE_NET_TRANS
WHERE dtperiod < GETUTCDATE() - 10
```

> If rows are returned from the preceding query that were older than 11 days, then that would mean that grooming failed. If no rows are returned older than the 10 days, further investigation needs to be performed and you might start from taking a look at what, and how much, data is stored inside the particular table.

6. Now we can run this query to delete rows by increments of 100,000:

```
Declare @row int; cfl declare @date datetime; cfl set @date =
GETUTCDATE() - 10

Set @row = (select COUNT(*) from core_net_trans where dtperiod < @
date);

While @row <> 0

Begin

Delete top(100000) from core_net_trans where dtperiod < @date

Set @row = (select COUNT(*) from core_net_trans where dtperiod < @
date);

End;
```

7. We also need to reclaim the disk space after removing the unwanted rows. To do that, open SQL Server Management Studio and right-click on your EdgeSight database name. Here I have used `EdgeSight` as the name; hence, click on **EdgeSight | Tasks | Shrink | Files**.

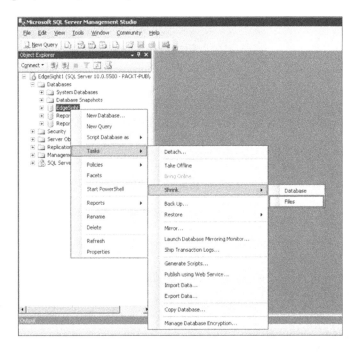

8. Select **FG6** as the **Filegroup** value and click on **OK**.

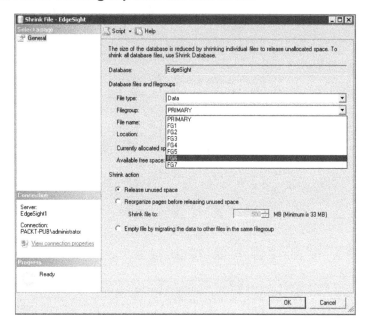

There's more...

You can also limit data uploads from the agents to the EdgeSight Server database by deselecting the type of performance data you are not interested in gathering. To configure these settings, navigate to **Configure | Server Configuration | Data Maintenance | Upload Configuration**.

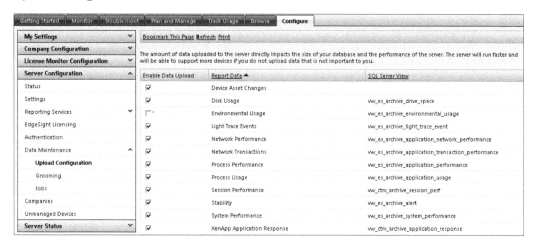

This also optimizes the EdgeSight Server performance.

About Packt Publishing

Packt, pronounced 'packed', published its first book "*Mastering phpMyAdmin for Effective MySQL Management*" in April 2004 and subsequently continued to specialize in publishing highly focused books on specific technologies and solutions.

Our books and publications share the experiences of your fellow IT professionals in adapting and customizing today's systems, applications, and frameworks. Our solution based books give you the knowledge and power to customize the software and technologies you're using to get the job done. Packt books are more specific and less general than the IT books you have seen in the past. Our unique business model allows us to bring you more focused information, giving you more of what you need to know, and less of what you don't.

Packt is a modern, yet unique publishing company, which focuses on producing quality, cutting-edge books for communities of developers, administrators, and newbies alike. For more information, please visit our website: www.packtpub.com.

Writing for Packt

We welcome all inquiries from people who are interested in authoring. Book proposals should be sent to author@packtpub.com. If your book idea is still at an early stage and you would like to discuss it first before writing a formal book proposal, contact us; one of our commissioning editors will get in touch with you.

We're not just looking for published authors; if you have strong technical skills but no writing experience, our experienced editors can help you develop a writing career, or simply get some additional reward for your expertise.

Citrix Access Gateway
VPX 5.04 Essentials

A practical step-by-step guide to provide secure remote access using the Citrix Access Gateway VPX

Andrew Mallett [PACKT] enterprise⊠

Citrix Access Gateway VPX 5.04 Essentials

ISBN: 978-1-84968-822-2   Paperback: 234 pages

A practical step-by-step guide to provide secure remote access using the Citrix Access Gateway VPX

1. A complete administration companion guiding you through the complexity of providing secure remote access using the Citrix Access Gateway 5 virtual appliance.

2. Establish secure access using ICA-Proxy to your Citrix XenApp and XenDesktop hosted environments.

3. Use SmartAccess technology to evaluate end users' devices before they connect to your protected network.

Citrix XenDesktop 5.6
Cookbook

Implement a fully featured XenDesktop 5.6 architecture in a rich and powerful VDI experience configuration

Gaspare A. Silvestri [PACKT] enterprise⊠

Citrix XenDesktop 5.6 Cookbook

ISBN: 978-1-84968-504-7   Paperback: 354 pages

Implement a fully featured XenDesktop 5.6 architecture in a rich and powerful VDI experience configuration

1. Real-world methodologies and functioning explanations about the XenDesktop 5.6 architecture and its satellite components used to perform a service-oriented architecture.

2. Learn how to publish desktops and applications to end user devices, optimizing their performance and increasing the general security.

3. Step-by-step guide on how to install and configure the XenDesktop 5.6 architecture to access and use the published virtual resources.

Please check **www.PacktPub.com** for information on our titles

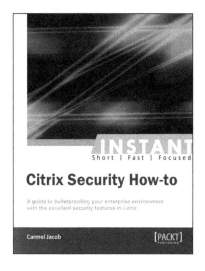

Instant Citrix Security How-to

ISBN: 978-1-84968-672-3   Paperback: 74 pages

A guide to bulletproofing your enterprise environment with the excellent security features in Citrix

1. Learn something new in an Instant! A short, fast, focused guide delivering immediate results.

2. Simple and detailed security implementations for your existing or brand new Citrix deployments.

3. Solutions to your network environment problems.

Instant Citrix XenApp

ISBN: 978-1-78217-026-6   Paperback: 50 pages

A short guide for administrators to get the most out of the Citrix XenApp 6.5 server farm

1. Learn something new in an Instant! A short, fast, focused guide delivering immediate results.

2. Plan, deploy, and manage a XenApp farm.

3. Learn how to manage resources in the farm through the use of graphical tools and PowerShell.

Please check **www.PacktPub.com** for information on our titles

www.ingramcontent.com/pod-product-compliance
Lightning Source LLC
LaVergne TN
LVHW080106070326
832902LV00014B/2462